Scenarios of Life

MICHAEL J GARDNER

AKA THE WALKING POET

FIRST EDITION

Published in 2025 by

GREEN CAT BOOKS

19 St Christopher's Way

Pride Park

Derby

DE24 8JY

www.greencatbooks.com

Copyright © 2025 Michael J Gardner

All rights reserved.

ISBN: 978-1-913794-85-9

No part of this publication

may be reproduced in any form or by any

means without the prior written permission of

the publisher.

This book is sold subject to the conditions that shall not, by way

of trade or otherwise, be lent, resold, hired out, or otherwise

circulated without the publisher's prior consent in any form of

binding other than that in which it is published and without a

similar condition including this condition being imposed on the

subsequent purchaser.

DEDICATION

For the support of folks at WMMC and South Wigston walking group

ACKNOWLEDGEMENTS

The Tree of Life image was painted by a survivor of head injury at
HEADWAY
Leicestershire, Leicester and Rutland day centre.

Parenthood

Ho, what joy! What can I say?
My wife delivered our child today.
I give love and thanks to my wife,
As we see our beautiful daughter come to life.

Through each breastfeed and nappy change,
And as our daughter grows, our lives we need to rearrange.
Then comes the time for the nursery run.
It's a joy to see her with other children having fun.

Those infant years seem so soon to be gone,
But we watch with pride, as she to junior school moves on.
Now it's study, exams and sport,
And requests for the latest gadgets to be bought.

And now to senior school she goes,
And with pride we watch our daughter, as she into a fine young lady grows.
Soon it's college, then a career,
Losing her to a busy life is what we fear.

So, dear daughter, this we say,
Don't totally go away.
When you're down or shed a tear,
Remember we so love you and are always here.

Piano

As my fingers glide across each piano key,
I feel the sense of love and passion flowing from the heart of me.

The music from my hands flies like a dove,
And glides across the land, a sign of peace and love.

I play a soft and gentle tune,
So touched are the hearts of folk, they begin to swoon.

Then I play aloud, with a crescendo for a treat.
It makes folks jump, and their hearts race and quicken beat.

The gift of music is placed within the heart.
It is a gift to be shared; a gift not to lose and from which we never want to part.

If music is the food of love,
Music comes from God above.

Let me learn to play the angels' song,
A song of peace and love, that I may share in the angelic throng.

Phoneless

I stand in the playground on my own.
No one notices me, because I haven't got a phone.
No one speaks or laughs with me,
For I'm not on social media, see.

X, Facebook and TikTok
Are the only interests that they've got.
If you are not on any of those,
The chance of friendship you seem to lose.

But when I hear of their fear and gloom,
As to them a site threatens their life and seeks to groom.
I am glad that I haven't got a phone,
And there's some value in being on your own.

Special Friendship

This love that doth burn so bright and so true,
Dearest friend, in friendship I freely give and offer you.
Our friendship means a lot to me.
I really treasure the time of friendship I share with thee.

It's been a long time since our friendship did start,
I only know that our friendship is a treasure to my heart.
As I remember the times we meet together, and in a greeting hug we hold,
I feel the warmth of friendship for you there unfold.

I'm blessed by the friendship and care you give,
You have brought a peace and beauty to the life I live.
I look forward to when we meet again,
You help ease my loneliness that causes me pain.

This friendship we have, to us such a gift,
Brings joy to our day and our spirits doth lift.
Let's treasure the moments of friendship together we share,
And remember its beauty as those memories in eternity will always dwell there.

Sweet Kisses

As I look at you, I see the beauty of your face,
And in your sparkling eyes, your soft and gentle love I trace.
And from your hand I feel your kind and gentle touch,
It thrills my heart and means so much.

You put your soft and tender lips to mine,
So sweet are your kisses, they taste like wine.
They are pure ecstasy, so of your kisses I take two,
For I feel so much love for you.

And as we hug face to face,
And with our arms around each other do embrace,
I feel the power of God's love untold,
Our loving union now enfold.

Valued by Society

I go through life without sight to see.
Who will come and care and be a guide for me?
I go through life unable to hear.
Who will come and sign for me, and make what's said to me more clear?

I go through life and can't move my arm or hand.
Who will come to help and understand?
I go through life without my legs, so cannot walk, only move my arms and speak.
Who will come and push my chair and give the fellowship I seek?

These questions are asked by folks each day,
But some folks seem to turn away.
Though folks may have a disability,
They have skills that should be valued by society.

Eternal Love

When our loved ones are seriously unwell,
Our hearts ache as doc says their future now, we cannot tell.
They do an examination, probe and a test,
To find the problem, they do their best.

The days and weeks go by so fast,
We try to keep our loved ones' spirits up, hoping our strength will last.
But then bad news makes us cry,
For we're told our loved one is so weak and soon to die.

But before our loved one passed away,
They had something to us to say.
"Remember, though my body doth this world depart,
My legacy of love for you will flow eternally within your heart."

Return Home

As we travel back from holiday,
We stop and enjoy a McDonald's on the way.
Then it's time to go back to the coach,
There's such a rush as we approach.

So once more we find our seat,
Now we relax and rest our feet.
We are weary and find it hard awake to keep,
So we finally fall asleep.

Then we feel the coach slow down,
And realise we're back in our home town.
We get our bag and our case,
And so for a taxi we do race.

As we go through our front door,
So glad to be home again once more.
As we share each photo and souvenir,
Family give us a hug and welcoming cheer.

Ode to Rob and Doddie

In the media and on TV,
We hear the tragic stories of folks with MND.
It takes away mobility and speech,
And for them a different kind of communication we need to teach.

Rob Burrows and Doddie Weir, the challenge, head on they met,
And Rob learned to speak with his eyes through the use of tech.
They are an inspiration to one and all,
Especially those who to the clutches of the dreaded MND do fall.

Sadly they are not with us now,
But they have left a legacy and how?
For through Doddie's foundation and Rob's centre built, their legacies left in their name,
The fighting spirit of Doddie and Rob lives on just the same.

Scenarios of Life

Within the scenarios of life in which we live,
Stress and pain take our strength and a lack of hope doth give,
Through the struggles of each day,
To buy our food and our bills to pay.

To put a roof above our head,
And even to give our child a bed,
Amidst the darkness of each day,
There are words that folks can say.

The words "WE CARE" and hold out a helping hand,
And show that they really understand.
To show the love within their heart,
Help us in rebuilding hope to make a start.

Within the scenarios of life,
It's not all pain; it's not all strife.
There are folks who love, and folks who care;
Give us hope and a brighter life in which to share.

This Drinking is a Problem

Down to the local disco with friends I go.
Together we groove and our dance moves we show.
We enjoy lots of drinks, music and dance,
But the drink gets too much, and I fall into a trance.

I staggered to the car, but my friends made a fuss.
"You're not driving tonight," they said, and put me on a bus.
The bus came and I climbed up the stair,
My friends said goodnight and gave the driver my fare.

I got off at my stop and walked to my flat.
I put the key in the door and as I entered I fell over the cat.
This drinking is a problem I really must solve,
I need real help to gain more resolve.

I speak to the AA for support and their care,
And at each session, with others the therapy share.
Moving on, without booze, the healthier I grow.
My need for the bottle I don't have in this new life that I know.

Christmas Lights

I watch the Christmas lights switch on tonight,
They twinkle like stars and shine so bright.
There's flashing stars, trees and reindeers too,
They bring such cheer and excitement as we our Christmas shopping do.

The Christmas tunes they play out loud,
And we sing along as we dodge and weave through the crowd.
The market stall holders shout joyfully to sell their wares,
to lift folks' spirits so they forget their cares.

Tis a time when we are kind to both friends or stranger,
And celebrate the Christ child as he lays in a manger.
We wish you love, joy and peace, we say,
And hope that they stay with you through your life each day.

Across the Universe

Here we drift in what is known as outer space.
No human mind knows its beginning nor its end can trace.
Each star we see, and at which we stare,
Twinkle from afar but may not be there.

Planets like deserts, planets like fire,
Planets so soft and seem like a mire.
Rocks and comets, meteorites and gases,
All come together to form Heaven's masses.

Across the universe there are mysteries untold,
Like blackholes, wormholes and other phenomena that time will unfold.
As planets explode and planets are born,
From the darkness comes wonder and magic as we see a new galaxy dawn.

Be a Good Samaritan

As I sat quietly at the bar
Drinking a refreshing jar,
A man came alongside and showed me pictures of past friends,
And spoke long of friendships he thought would never end.

Now sadly all his friends are gone, and he in memory only can join the throng.
He in grief begins to weep
And curls up awash in tears upon the seat.

I wondered why I was there,
Why he chose me his pain to share.
Am I to be his Good Samaritan today,
And help in this life to stay?

To speak with care and to him give hope,
So that through grief he'll find a way to cope,
When I left, he had a friend with whom his joys and woes could share.
A friend who shows kindness and Christian care.

Beauty of an Empty Street

As I walk along this empty street,
Both peace and silence are all I meet.
The shops with all their shutters down,
Their architecture, the street with beauty crown.

No children play and no folks to rush about,
And no loud voices there to shout.
The cash dispensers in silence lay,
No balance to show or cash to pay.

And along the street the sun begins to rise and shine,
It brings such joy and blessing to this heart of mine.
Whether in rain or sun,
It brings joy to me as each day as begun.

Breaker, Breaker, S O S

We went for a walk up that hill yesterday,
But near to the top we both lost our way
So I moved to the edge,
And between two rocks, myself I did wedge.

I took out my CB radio and shouted breaker, breaker, S.O.S,
Can someone rescue us because we're in a mess.
The helicopter came and hovered above,
The paramedic drifted down, just like a dove.

And so we are down safely now,
And with our heartfelt thanks we give them a bow.
For from our dilemma they safely did scoop,
And now here they are giving us tea and a hot bowl of soup.

Broken Hearted 💔

Yesterday you said you loved me, and by my side you'd stay.
But today you leave me, and with someone else's emotions play.
Although I love you dearly, I know your love is not true,
If it was, you'd stay with me, and together we'd live our whole life through.

If you give false affection, and proclaim it to one and all,
You'll finish with such loneliness and head for a fall.
Although I really love you, you caused my broken heart.
It's me who now leaves you. For us there is no future, it's best if we're apart.

Can't Find the Words

To my family and friends, I want to speak,
But sadly, I can't find the words that within my mind I seek.
I think of words from A to Zee,
But the one I want won't come to me.

Some folks get impatient and unkind,
Because I struggle with words to find.
Their actions make me struggle even more to think.
My confidence is shattered and begins to sink.

But family and friends are really grand,
Because my dilemma, they understand.
They will coax and guide me so,
And help me find the word that I want to know.

I ask that you kindly show patience too,
For one day it could happen to you.
I hope, for you, that folks are kind,
And understand more about the fragility of the mind.

Christmas Frenzy

The Christmas frenzy now begins,
And folks dash from store to store as a choir sings.
The Christmas tree is lit and shines so bright,
And with the street decorations, makes a wonderful sight.

Folks buy their food and presents too,
And remember friends like Jack and Sue.
All this shopping disrupts the festive fair,
As we remember folks who won't be there.

Like family deceased or far away,
We get a wreath or card to express our love, and with written words to say.
Tis a time for children too,
To see their joy as they play is a blessing to folks, that is so true.

But sadly, this is not true for all,
For there are folks who have to sleep against a sheltered wall.
No one knows what pain they see,
Their plight is ignored by society.

So as we open presents and eat our food,
And together play in festive mood,
Let's remember those who sleep out in the cold,
And suffer and die before they get old.

Cloud Control

We awake today to find our system down,
It causes folks to stress, panic and give a frustrated frown.
No planes can fly, or buses run,
We can't travel, and without a screen it's no fun.

Our dependency upon the cloud
Covers our lives like a shroud.
When it fails and is not there,
We are lost, as at empty screens we stare.

Sometimes the old ways are the best,
Against system failure they stand the test.
Once back up systems were in place,
We could, up to the point of failure our data trace.

The moral of this story that I make,
Is for folks appropriate precautions so to take
For eggs all in one basket when it has a fall,
It doesn't just break one it affects them all.

Daily Rush

Off today again I rush
Down the lane to catch the bus.
As I get on the bus and pay my fare,
I greet my friends as we, together this journey share.

I am enjoying speaking to Liz and Pam,
I barely notice the traffic jam.
We say our farewells as we depart,
Then the rush to work I start.

And as I deal with the pressures of the day that are a pain,
I look forward to getting on the bus again.
To be away from the crowd
And not hear folks who shout so loud.

Ho to be back at home,
As I give my dog's fur a gentle comb.
Now from stress I feel free,
And now I can enjoy my cup of tea.

Friend like a Pearl

My friend, I am glad that you are here,
As we talk and walk you help my loneliness disappear.
You share in fun and laughter, and kindness too.
This is the treasure that is you.

You help and say words of comfort when I shed a tear.
I'm glad I have a friend who shows kindness and comforts me to ease my fear.

You came in my distress and darkest hour
Into my life you did kindness and compassion shower.
Our friendship I will always treasure,
It's a precious gift beyond all measure.

Our friendship, like a pearl, it dwells within my heart,
As I go through life, it's a treasure from which I never want to part.

Heaven's Beauty

Up in this spaceship to the heavens I'm hurled,
I look down through the window at the beautiful world.
As I drift towards the space station, for it's there that is my destination
I think this journey on which I go will be the most beautiful trip that I'll ever know.

As I dock at the hatch and go through the door,
There's no more gravity, so I float up from the floor.
I'm now here at my destination,
And working with folks from many a nation.

And when comes the time for me to depart,
These strangers, now friends, will remain in my heart.
Now to them all I say my goodbyes
And prepare to fly back to the world's cloudy skies.

And now I've returned here on the earth's ground,
I'll always remember that journey, and the beauty of the heavens up there that I found.

I Tend the Garden

I go out to tend the garden to cast away the bugs and weeds,
And then to plant the seasonal seeds.

I tend the roses, these majestic flowers,
As each upon the air their fragrance showers.

The fruit hangs brightly on the trees,
Their colours tempt us and our tastebuds tease.

There comes a gentle shower,
That enables plants to grow and trees to tower.

It fills the pond and cleans the path,
And leaves fresh air as its aftermath.

And having laboured through the day,
Back into the house I make my way.

A wash of hand and of knee,
Then I sit down and enjoy my cup of tea.

Let the Dementia Choir Sing

Ho let the dementia choir sing,
That they to fellow sufferers, hope do bring.
The music speaks to the sub conscience of their mind,
So again their special songs they find.

For as they sing their favourite song,
It helps bring memories of love and family to the fore, where they belong.
I hope for all with dementia the music continues to play,
So love to friends and family they can once more know and say.

MOT Test

I've come to the garage for an MOT,
Hoping for a clear sheet to see.
Sitting there with not much to do,
And only a shop window to look through.
I look around the showroom cars,
As I check out the price, my mind it jars.

I go back to my seat with a sweet cup of tea,
Having seen the prices, I'm in shock, you see.
The car that I have is a good little car,
And when I drive it is the best experience for me by far.
I drive down county lanes, and cruise round the bends,
Such moments of pleasure and excitement to me does it lend.

The mechanic comes back with test sheet,
And good news to me he gives as we greet.
Your car has passed its MOT test,
That news soothes my mind and puts it to rest.
MOT, the stress and anxiety that these things can bring,
The words, "It's passed" make your heart sing.

My Fear

Off to the surgery for my COVID shot,
I try to control the fear of needles that I've got.

I shout, scream and curse,
Then I apologise to the nurse.

This fear I've had since I was a child,
As I get older, it still drives me wild.

Is there a way forward to cope with this stress?
For of my life it's made such a mess.

The stress and the pain have driven my fears,
Sometimes I can't help but to burst into tears.

Through my life all this has caused me such shame,
I can think of no cause, but me do I blame.

If you can help and bring me some hope,
To overcome my fears, then with life learn to cope.

New Hope

Each day there are parents who lose their child,
Within their hearts the questions, pain and grief run wild.
Each night they do not sleep but have turned and tossed,
As they are haunted by the battle for life their child has lost.

How will they cope with the emptiness each day?
No more can they see their child at work or play.
Friends and family bring their love, encouragement and hope,
And together find the way forward each day to cope.

Let's fight the cause of the loss of a child and the grieving that the parents know,
Start a charity in the child's name, seek a law or research so that others do not suffer so.
Help them turn their grief into positivity,
To give to others encouragement and new hope to see.

New Year Challenges

As we come again to the new year,
Do we face it with joy or is it with fear?
Do we go forth with a heart full of hope,
Or doubt our ability with its challenges to cope?

Look around at your family and your friends,
And remember that for you their love never ends.
With good family and friends in your life,
You will travel together through the joy and the strife.

What gift do we have in this new year?
It is the treasure of family and friends, that within our hearts we hold dear.
Friendship and love are the pearls that bring hope,
And gives us the strength with new year challenges to cope.

Now Break Free

We seem to be governed by tech today,
Without the phone we wouldn't know what to do or say.
Each day we hop into the car,
Whether it's to the shop or travelling far.

I wonder if one day we'll forget how to walk,
And person to person how to talk.
Distant communication and sedentary travel,
Will it make our society unravel?

Social media has its say, and brings not only joy but lots of pain,
And influence on your life to gain.
Let's build a person to person community
And from social media, now break free.

Our Child is Autistic

Our child is autistic and it begins to show
As the challenges of the world she comes to know.

She asks the question, "Is it me or is it they
Who live their lives a different way?"

Our child needs routine in her day,
And in small talk, doesn't have much to say.

Meeting people must be planned,
Crowded places in her mind are banned.

In her mind she seeks some focus,
Like maps, puzzles and aerial photos.

Sometimes folks are ignorant and unkind,
And a lack of understanding is what we find.

Our child may have, of life, a different view,
But needs love and care like me and you.

Our Wedding Day

We are so happy now,
For we have each made our wedding vow.
And share the encouragement of family and friends,
And feel their love that never ends.

Now as we go down the lane and depart,
And the drifting of confetti start.
We say our fond farewell,
The folks give their best wishes and of their love for us do tell.

We thank you all who came to share,
We love the fact that you were there.
We go now, to share our life,
To share the blessing of being husband and wife.

Remember the Fallen

Remember the fallen of wars of the past,
Their service great, and sacrifices ho so vast.
Remember the fallen of today,
Those who serve in lands so far away.

Let's remember those who, their lives do give,
And give thanks to them for the days of peace in which we live.
On this and each Remembrance Day,
Let not our memories of them, nor our thanks ever fade away.

For all who serve, and defend our nation,
We on this day join in a thankful celebration.
We give thanks in music and in song,
And share our memories of our fallen loved ones, memories that today still live on.

Sands of Time

As I walk each day through the sands of time,
I suffer in sadness and treasure the sublime.
The sadness is loss, pain and grief,
All of which challenges one's hope and belief.

The sublime is friendship, love and joy,
And the beauty of new life, be it a girl or boy.
The beauty of love from hearts so entwined,
Just like the love in our hearts, that together we find.

We treasure through time the moments that for us are meant,
But remember that from eternity those moments are lent.
Love and compassion, together a mark in eternity stamp,
They become like a star, and shine like a lamp.

Saved Her Tears

I come to this café for a bite,
And watch the cars trying to beat the traffic light.
I watch folks running across the road,
Carrying shopping or a heavy load.

Friends come in and to me they kindly speak,
And with me they take a seat.
And in conversation talk
About the beauty of our latest walk.

Then suddenly there's a screech of brakes
And as we look upon the scene, our breath it takes.
An elderly lady crossing the road,
Her bag had split and spilled its load.

Folks rushed to help her out,
Some just stood and at the driver shout.
The kindness that those folks gave
Helped ease her stress and her tears did save.

Seek Changes

I awake each day with my troubles and strife,
So much so I don't know what to do with my life.

I ask my boss to give me a sub
I finish up spending it down at the pub.

My friends tell me if I keep at the booze,
The only thing gained is for my life to lose.

So, I seek to change as from today,
And admit my weakness to the folks at AA.

And now with their help, a better future before me,
now I can see.
Thanks to my friends and folks at AA for the care
and the kindness freely given to me.

Sitting on a Fence

As I sit upon this fence and stare,
I see a lass slowly walking in the distance there.
The grass, so gentle her journey made.
Beyond the majestic trees their branches from sun and rain they shade.

Out from the tall grass her dogs doth bark,
Now I see them chase a ball and play and lark.
Tis a lovely sight to see,
It is a real joy to me.

The lass walks to me now with lively pace,
I see the beauty of the smile upon her face.
We open arms, each to embrace,
We feel the love as we touch face to face.

This is my love from Lancashire,
I've waited so long to meet her here.
Now together we go on,
For our hearts will forever sing our love song.

The Chair

Each day I go out in my wheelchair.
I go to the shops and get out in the open air.
As I travel along the street,
Some folks prejudiced to me I meet.

Folk above and around me speak,
As I with them, conversation seek.
They look at me and stare
And all they see is the chair.

I am the same as you - I eat, drink and talk.
There is no difference even though I cannot walk.
I am glad my family and friends don't stare,
And they see me and not the chair.

The Final Cut

We meet again on this sunny day,
On the course our golf to play.
We spin to see who's first, you or me,
You win and take your place upon the tee.

You place your ball and make your shot.
When it lands, I'm amazed how far it got.
I take my turn and make my swing,
It flies through the air, and as it lands, ho yes, I sing.

As we walk from green to green,
And take in the beauty of the scene,
My score is close to what you've got,
There's just one hole to take top spot.

The tension is high as this swing I take,
Hoping that a birdie I make.
Then you are on the tee,
Hoping to the winner be.

Your second shot is somewhat poor,
You're disappointed and feel so sore.
On the green we both make our final putt.
We half the hole, and joy of joys, we both make the final cut.

The Love That is Betwixt Us

Ho, what love from thee doth fly to me and pierce my heart and soul,
And my love I give to thee, not in part, I give it to thee whole.
The love that is betwixt us around our hearts doth entwine,
And fills our life with beauty, both yours and mine.

And as we walk and talk and travel through life each day,
Our love, its beauty and its treasure grows along the way.
My dearest sweetheart, our love is so beautiful, more than I dreamt that it could ever be.
I just seek to tell thee, our love will always dwell within the heart of me.

They Show Me Love

In giving birth, Mum suffered pain that stopped her heart,
And so to heaven she did depart.

Sadly, Mum's life ended as I came into the world so meek and mild,
She didn't get to see her lovely child.

Folks took me in and gave me love and care,
But I really missed my mum who was not there.

I had an attitude and sometimes wild,
And sometimes folks thought I was a problem child.

But over time love won through,
And I learned from my heart to love them too.

To me they became like Mum and Dad,
They show me love and care, and comfort me when I'm sad.

I say if you've been through this too, have hope, for there are folks who have a loving, caring heart,
And that love and care to you impart.

Today is Not a Good Start

Today is not a good start,
For bad news doth cause pain within my heart.
My sister is not well, my best friend has left
And I don't know what to do for the best.

How with this heartache now do I cope?
Where do I search for that blessing called hope?
Dear Lord, please guide me to where help I can find,
Perhaps a Good Samaritan who's caring and kind.

That with them I can share the pains in my heart,
And they to me some kind wisdom impart.
I went out to a café at the end of the street,
And sat with a drink hoping some friends I would meet.

My prayers were answered as a friend came in,
And from my friend's kind words to me begin.
I feel now more able to cope,
My friend's words helped me find the blessing called hope.

Treasure of Weather

Today the rain it pours,
So we refrain from going outdoors.
The clouds, now they go, here comes the sun,
And we rush out to brown like a currant bun.

Today the frost makes patterns on the windowpane,
It's so cold out there, it causes pain.
So back into our warm armchair we slink,
Then enjoy a luscious chocolate drink.

Today the snow falls on the ground,
Falling soft and gentle it makes no sound.
And as I go home to get my lunch,
With every step I take, I leave my footprints as I hear them crunch.

About the weather we complain,
We moan about the frost, the wind and rain.
If the weather wasn't so,
The plants and nature would not grow.

Trip to Town

As I get the bus to go to town,
The folks I see give a smile, turn away or just frown.

The scene from the window goes by so fast,
My time on the bus is so quickly passed.

I'm off the bus and into the shops, some folks rush out when they see the cops.
They are quickly caught as a taser pops.

All this activity makes me shake and then to cry,
With the shock I cannot speak but only sigh.

A kind lady brings me a drink,
It helps me to chill and time to think.

Voting Time

Ho dear, it's that time again to vote,
When folks say a lot, but really say nowt.

They sit on tractor, boat or plane,
Some of their stunts seem quite insane.

They come around to your door,
They speak politely as they seek to know who you'll vote for.

On TV we see their banners red, blue, orange and green;
The only colourful part in this political scene.

No matter who loses or who wins,
Folks will point out their political sins.

As the bills and laws for us are made,
Would we, for a different outcome, our choice now trade?

But having made our final choices,
We hope they'll continue to listen to our voices.

We Preach Out There in the Street

We preach out there in the street,
Folks gather round and with us, meet.

We preach there that God's gospel should be heard,
And that folks shall understand his every word.

We preach out there, and with hymns we sing,
And confess our heartfelt love of Christ within.

We preach out there to reach each lost soul,
And share communion that they today can be made whole.

We preach out there, we have no brick church,
And no seats on which to perch.

But what we have is faith and love,
And a desire for you to know our Lord above.

To spread Christ's gospel is our goal,
And that his truth may touch your heart and save your soul.

We Walk Together

I'm meeting my friends for a walk today.
We greet each other with hugs, and share in conversation on the way.

We walk together through the country park,
In friendship laugh and have a lark.

The group together are like family,
They really mean so much to me.

They are the treasure of my day.
From the heart "I love you all" to them I say.

A better group of friends I do not know,
And I treasure the friendship and the love that, to me they show.

What is This?

What is this life to which we're born,
As we leave the womb to greet the dawn.
What is this that we feel as we lay in mother's arms,
And that we see upon her face as she looks upon our facial charms?

As we grow to understand,
Tis love we feel from her heart and given by her caring hand.
Mother and Father teach us how with life's challenges to cope,
And speak to us of love and hope.

But as we rebel within our teens,
It's hard to tell what their love for us really means.
But when we find love and family of our own,
We understand the treasured love that from birth to us was shown.

Winter Now Comes

Winter now comes round again,
And with it comes such fear and strain.
As we struggle to pay for winter fuel,
Deciding between food or heat is now our seasonal duel.

No fires lit, no heating on,
O how soon my funds are gone.
Trapped under this duvet with a tear,
As I the cruelty of this winter fear.

I'm on my own in this cold house,
Hibernating like a dormant mouse.
Don't know what I'm going to live on,
For my meager funds will soon be gone.

What can I do to survive?
Will government help my funds revive?
I don't ask for the world, no not a lot,
Just help to keep us warm and a quality to the life we've got.

About The Author

I'm Michael J Gardner Aka The Walking Poet. Why The Walking Poet, you ask. Well I am a volunteer wellbeing walk leader for my local borough council. But when I started with the group I was prescribed to it by a Social Prescriptive Link Worker after my wife died. The group was the best place for me, they helped a lot.

When I was working I was a safety rep, and when I was mid 60s I trained as a Lay Preacher, my poems are written in the way they are because I write what I feel. And writing that way these poems I share with you have been a good therapy to get me through my grief. I am now a volunteer for Leicestershire, Leicester and Rutland Headway.

Other Books by Michael

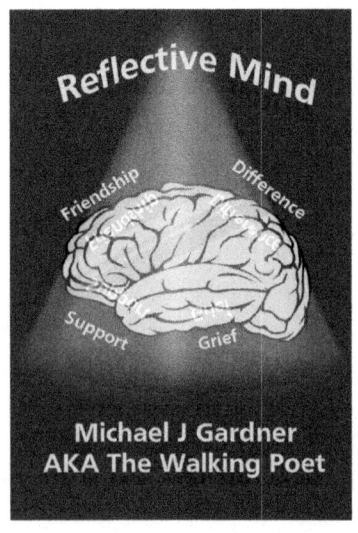

For more information about our books and services, please visit

www.greencatbooks.com

Printed in Great Britain
by Amazon